Delicious Tater Tot Meals to Wet Your Appetite in Every Way You Can Imagine!

I Love Tater Tots

THE LEGAL PAGE

DISCLAIMER: This book is independently published by, and is **not** affiliated with, sponsored by, or endorsed by any of the products mentioned in this book. All other company and product names are the trademarks of their respective owners. The author reserves the right to make any changes he or she deems necessary to future versions of the publication to ensure its accuracy.

Special Notes for the Recipes in this Book: The recipes in this book may include raw eggs. Raw eggs may contain bacteria. It is recommended that you purchase certified salmonella-free eggs from a reliable source and store them in the refrigerator. You should not feed raw eggs to babies or small kids. Likewise, pregnant women, elderly persons, or those with a compromised immune system should not eat raw eggs. Neither the author nor the publisher claims responsibility for adverse effects resulting from the use of the recipes and/or information found within this book.

The information contained in this book is for entertainment purposes only. The author does not assume any liability whatsoever for the use of or inability to use any or all information contained in this book, and accepts no responsibility for any loss or damages of any kind that may be incurred by the reader as a result of actions arising from the use of the information in this book. The content represents the opinion of the author and is based on the author's personal experience and observations.

Use this information at your own risk. No part of this book may be reproduced or transmitted in any form or by any means, electronic or mechanical, including photocopying, recording, or by any information storage or retrieval system, without express written permission from the author, except in the case of brief quotations embodied in critical articles and reviews – or except by a reviewer who may quote brief passages in a review.

Respective authors hold all copyrights not held by the publisher
COPYRIGHT © 2018, Alicia Patterson All Rights Reserved.
Published in The United States of America

Alicia Patterson

INTRO MESSAGE

It all started with an idea from a potato... and now we present to you, the tater tot! All the different ways you can enjoy this delicious potato nugget is in this book right in front of you! We made it fun, simple and easy to understand language that makes it fun for not only you but your family to get involved as well. Your kids are just going to love you to pieces! These are some of the most creative tater tot recipes that you'll get out of any cookbook out there!

We show you ways of making tater tots that you've never thought of before. Did you know that there are tater tots made from other vegetables besides potatoes? This book is full of wonderful surprises double spruce up any meal that you make with these recipes in your kitchen!

You will love this book so much that you'll even get your kids involved in making these great tasting potato nuggets that everyone will enjoy! Read review these pages and you'll see why!

I Love Tater Tots

The Legal Page — *2*

Intro Message — *3*

Tottin' Like a Tot Junkie! — *8*
We Loves Tots and You Do Too!!! — 8

The Skill & Craft, It's Perfect — *9*
Crafting the Perfect Tater Tots — 9

Any Way You Want Em'! — *10*
Cooking Methods to Make You Look Like a Pro — 10

Golden Brown, How I Like Em' — *11*
Golden Brown, a Light Crisp and Soft in the Middle — 11

25 Recommended Dips! ☺ — *12*

The Choice is Yours! — *14*
Regular or Breaded Balls…It's Up to You! — 14

Dip Em' and Dunk Em' — *16*
Loaded Tater Tot Dip — 16
Slam Dunk Tot Sauce — 17
Soy Chili Tot Sauce — 18
Spicy Jalapeño Horseradish Tot Sauce — 19
Spicy Garlic Mayo Tot Dipper — 20

Pork'Em Up — *21*
Carolina Style Pulled Pork Tater Tot Bites — 21
Tater Tot Cups with Cheese and Bacon — 22
Cheesy Ranch Bacon Tater Tot Skewers — 23
Bacon and Cheese Sriracha Tater Tots — 24
Bacon and Sausage Nacho Tots — 25
Tennessee Pulled Pork Barbecue Tater Tot Nachos — 26
Pulled Pork Tater Tots with Fontina — 27
Tater Tots Bacon Cheeseburger Style — 28

Cheesy Breakfast Tater Tots with Bacon	29
Southern Cheesy Bacon Tater Tot Bites	30

Nothin but the Beef...& Tots — 31

Cowboy Tater Tots	31
Cheeseburger Tater Tot Cups	32
Chili Dog Tater Tots	33
Philly Cheesesteak Tater Tots	34
Ground Beef Taco Tater Tots	35
Greek Tater Tot Nachos	36
Tater Tot Beef Dip	37

For the Vegetarians — 38

Cheesy Ranch Tater Tots	38
Chipotle Tater Tot Nachos	39
Garlic and Cheese Tater Tot Bundt	40
Rosemary Tater Tot with Malt Vinegar Dipping Sauce	41
Asian BBQ Tater Tots	42
Parmesan Tater Tots	43
Cheesy Buffalo Tater Tots	44
Thyme Tater Tot with Ranch Dressing	45
Cajun Tater Tots	46
Old Bay Tater Tots	47
Taco Flavored Tater Tots	48
Smokey Paprika Tater Tots with Chipotle Ketchup	49
Buffalo Ranch Tater Tots	50
Feta Tater Tots	51
Italian Seasoned Tater Tots	52
Jalapeno Popper Tater Tots	53
Korean Ginger and Garlic Tater Tots with Spicy Cheese Sauce	54

Chicken — 55

Chicken Tater Tot Casserole	55
Ranch Cheesy Chicken Tater Tot Casserole	56
Double Cheesy Chicken Tater Tot Casserole	57
Buffalo Chicken Tater Tot Skillet	58

Chicken and Stuffing Tater Tot Casserole	59
Mexican Chicken and Tater Tot Casserole	60
Chicken Tender and Cheese Tater Tot Casserole	61
Chicken Pot Pie Tater Tot Casserole	62
Chicken Broccoli Cheddar Tater Tot Casserole	63
Chicken Fajita Breakfast Tater Tot Casserole	64
Southwestern Tater Tot Casserole	65

Sweet Potato Tots — 66

Sweet Potato Tater Tot Casserole	66
Sweet Potato Tater Tot Nachos	67
Rosemary Thyme and Sea Salt Sweet Potato Tater Tots	68
Paprika and Thyme Sweet Potato Tater Tots	69
Sweet and Spicy Sweet Potato Tater Tots	70
Cajun Spiced Sweet Potato Tater Tots	71
Cumin Chili Powder and Garlic Sweet Potato Tater Tots	72
Moroccan Spiced Sweet Potato Tater Tots	73
Za'atar Sweet Potato Tater Tots with Tahini Dip Sauce	74
Herbs De Provence Sweet Potato Tater Tots	75
Indian Spiced Sweet Potato Tater Tots	76
Greek Inspired Sweet Potato Tater Tots	77
Dijon Sweet Potato Tater Tots	78
Spanish Spiced Sweet Potato Tater Tots	79
Mexican Inspired Sweet Potato Tater Tots	80

Tater Tots for Dessert — 81

Churro Tater Tots with Dulce De Leche Sauce	81
Apple Tater Tot Crisp	82
Chocolate Covered Bacon Wrapped Tater Tots	83
Cinnamon Sugar Sweet Potato Tater Tots	84
Tater Tots with Chocolate Peppermint Icing and Crushed Candy Canes	85
Chocolate Covered Tater Tots with Shredded Coconut	86
White Chocolate "Birthday Cake" Tater Tots	87
Cookies and Cream Tater Tots	88
Peanut Butter Chocolate Tater Tots	89

Chocolate Covered Tater Tots with Caramel and Sea Salt   *90*
White Chocolate Macadamia Nut Sweet Potato Tater Tots   *91*
Milk Chocolate Pretzel Tater Tots   *92*
Dark Chocolate Almond Sweet Potato Tater Tots   *93*
S'mores Sweet Potato Tater Tots   *94*
Dark Chocolate Pistachio Sweet Potato Tater Tots   *95*

About Our Author   96

TOTTIN' LIKE A TOT JUNKIE!
We Loves Tots and You Do Too!!!

Tater tots are an American classic. They take us back to our childhood, when the lunch lady would serve them to us. There's nothing better than a grilled cheese and a side of crispy, golden tater tots. Tater tots are so much tastier than their French fry siblings.

Tater tots are crunchy on the outside and oh so soft on the inside. They're like crunchy clouds of perfection that are perfect for dipping. French fries don't give you the satisfying crunch that tots do. Tot are incredibly versatile too. You can eat them on their own, topped them with different ingredients, and even make them into a casserole. If you don't love tots, you will after this book.

Alicia Patterson

THE SKILL & CRAFT, IT'S PERFECT
Crafting the Perfect Tater Tots

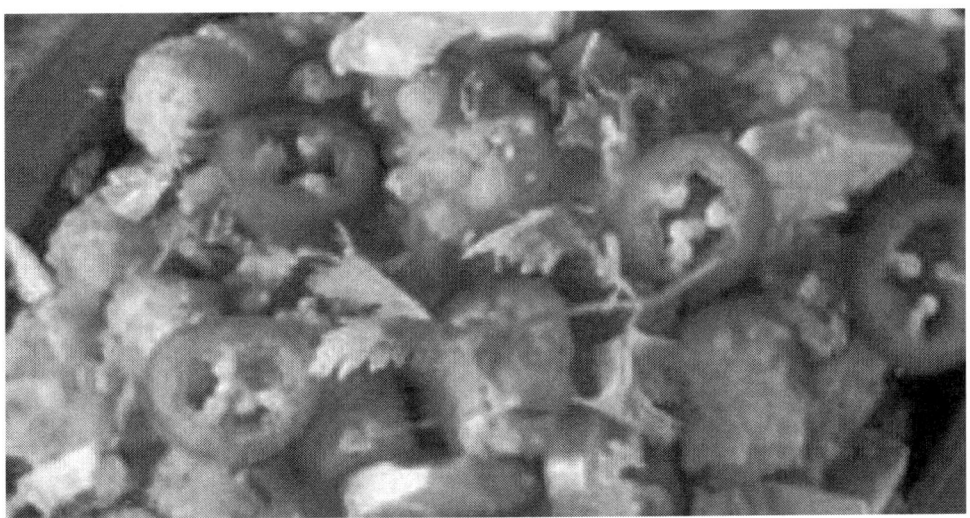

Crafting the perfect tots is a personal experience. Everyone has different tastes and tots can be made to fit those tastes. You can season them simply, add meats and cheeses, and even make them sweet. There's a whole world of flavors for you to explore.

Get creative with your thoughts and try something you never tried before. Combine your favorite ingredients to make a tater tot masterpiece. Your belly will thank you when you're done.

ANY WAY YOU WANT EM'!
Cooking Methods to Make You Look Like a Pro

Pan Fry Em':

Place   cup of the oil of your choice in a big skillet and heat on medium-high heat. Fry the tots for 6 to 10 minutes, flipping halfway through.

Oven Bake Em':

Preheat your oven to 425F. Use cooking spray to coat a baking sheet. Place the tater tots on the baking sheet. Bake the tots for about 25 minutes. They should be nice and crispy.

Deep Fry Em:

Pour the oil of your choice into your deep fryer. Heat the oil to 375F and fry the tater tots for 6 to 10 minutes.

Air Fry Em':

Spray the basket of your air fryer with cooking spray and preheat the air fryer to 400F. Put the tots in the basket of your air fryer and cook for 8 to 10 minutes.

Alicia Patterson

GOLDEN BROWN, HOW I LIKE EM'
Golden Brown, a Light Crisp and Soft in the Middle

The crispy exterior is the best part of the tater tots. A crispy exterior makes the soft interior so much better. It adds a beautiful contrast of textures.

If your tots aren't crispy enough cook them for a couple extra minutes. Always keep an eye on them, because it's easy for them to burn. A watchful eye will ensure sure you walk the line of super crispy and burned.

25 RECOMMENDED DIPS! ☺

Thousand Island Dressing and Ketchup
It just works!

Brown Gravy
If you can put it on mashed potatoes then you can use it to dip tater tots

Melted Cheese
(Any kind but Queso is best! Yummm! :)

Marinara Sauce
Move over Spaghetti…Tots are here to dip!.

Mexican Style Mayonnaise (Mayo + Sriracha)
Trust me…It's just good!

Guacamole
Usually for tortilla chips…now for tater tots!

Spicy Mustard
Spicy mustard just does something to the tots!

Ranch Dressing
We've all done this before!

Buffalo Sauce
Dip your tots in the sauce while eating those Buffalo wings!

Ranch Dressing & Buffalo Sauce
This combination will make you say Mmmmmmm!

Hot Sauce + Honey
Simple to mix and great to eat!

Barbecue Sauce
You don't have to grill your tots, but the BBQ sauce is fabulous!

Alicia Patterson

Sweet-N-Sour Sauce
You'll think you're dipping egg rolls but better!

Caramel sauce
Don't knock it till you try it!

Duck Sauce
Always have leftover packets in your kitchen.

Thai-Style Sweet Chili Sauce
The honey hot and sweet taste of the Orient.

Salsa
Not just for the tortilla chip!

Bacon Jam
Bacon just goes with everything!

Sour Cream & Onion Dip
Don't miss out on this one. Delicious!

Steak Sauce
Instead of steak and fries…steak and tots!

Malt Vinegar
Instead of fish & chips…fish & tots! (and yes…add the malt vinegar)

Worcestershire Sauce
It's not just for steaks and it's Ohhhh, Soooo, Gooood!.

Garlic Hummus
Save your pitas for gyros.

Vanilla Milkshakes
Oh boy…yummy.

Poached Eggs
(Dip em' in the yolk)

THE CHOICE IS YOURS!
Regular or Breaded Balls...It's Up to You!

Get ready for flavor explosion in your mouth and belly. The recipes in this book will surely satisfy your palette. We've got recipes for people that love meat, vegetarian, sweet potato tater tots, and even dessert tots. No matter what you're looking for we've got a recipe for you. There are recipes that work as a side dish and others that work as a main course. We've got you covered for breakfast, lunch, dinner, and beyond.

So, get ready to give your taste buds a delicious work out. We've got some great recipes waiting for you.

Alicia Patterson

DIP EM' AND DUNK EM'

Loaded Tater Tot Dip

Prep Time: 10 Min. / **Cook Time:** 25 Min. / **Servings:** 6-8

Ingredients

45 -50 tater tots (about 3 cups) thawed
1 cup cooked, ground beef
2 cups shredded cheese
16 oz. sour cream
2 tsp all-purpose seasoning
Salt and pepper to taste

Directions:

- Preheat oven to 375F
- Use a 2-quart casserole baking dish and spray it with cooking spray.
- Cut each tater tot in half and put into a large mixing bowl. Add the ground beef (cooked of course), 1 cup of the mixed cheese, sour cream, seasoning blend. Mix all ingredients together.
- Pour the mix into the casserole dish. Add the rest of the cheese on top. Should be 1 cup.
- Bake for about 25 minutes. (or until golden brown)
- This dip works best with chips, crackers or even vegetables!
- Enjoy

Slam Dunk Tot Sauce

Prep Time: 10 Min. / **Cook Time:** 25 Min. / **Servings:** 6-8

Ingredients
1 cup ketchup
¼ cup mayonnaise
1 tbsp. pickle relish (sweet)
Salt and pepper to taste

Directions:
- Take a bowl for dipping the tater tots and pour the ketchup and mayonnaise and mix together.
- Then add the pickle relish to the mix. Stir the mix until it is mixed well together.
- Add salt and pepper to taste
- Start dipping and enjoy

Soy Chili Tot Sauce

Prep Time: 10 Min. / **Cook Time:** 25 Min. / **Servings:** 6-8

Ingredients
1 cup ketchup
¼ cup mayonnaise
1 tbsp. soy sauce
1 tsp. chili powder
Salt and pepper to taste

Directions:
- Take a bowl for dipping the tater tots and pour the ketchup and mayonnaise and mix together.
- Then add the soy and chili powder to the mix. Stir until it is mixed well together.
- Add salt and pepper to taste
- Start dipping and enjoy

Spicy Jalapeño Horseradish Tot Sauce

Prep Time: 10 Min. / **Cook Time:** 25 Min. / **Servings:** 6-8

Ingredients
1 cup ketchup
¼ cup mayonnaise
1 tbsp. jalapeño
½ tsp. horseradish
Salt and pepper to taste

Directions:
- Take a bowl for dipping the tater tots and pour the ketchup and mayonnaise and mix together.
- Then add the jalapeño and horseradish to the mix.
- Stir until it is mixed well together.
- Add salt and pepper to taste
- Start dipping and enjoy

Spicy Garlic Mayo Tot Dipper

Prep Time: 10 Min. / **Cook Time:** 25 Min. / **Servings:** 6-8

Ingredients
Sauce
1 teaspoon Garlic powder
1/2 cup Mayonnaise
4 tablespoons Pickle relish
2 tablespoons Yellow mustard
1 teaspoon White wine vinegar
1 teaspoon Paprika
1 teaspoon Onion powder

Directions:
- Take a bowl for dipping the tater tots and pour the ketchup and mayonnaise and mix together.
- Then add the jalapeño and horseradish to the mix.
- Stir until it is mixed well together.
- Add salt and pepper to taste
- Start dipping and enjoy

PORK'EM UP

Carolina Style Pulled Pork Tater Tot Bites

Prep Time: 10 Min. / **Cook Time:** 30 Min. / **Servings:** 8

Ingredients:
1, 2-pound bag tater tots
2 cups shredded cooked pork
1 1/2 cups coleslaw cabbage blend
2 Tablespoons Apple Cider Vinegar
1 Tablespoon Mayonnaise
1 Tablespoon Yellow Mustard
1/2 cup Carolina style BBQ Sauce

Directions:
- Preheat your oven to 425F. Use parchment to line a baking sheet.
- Put the tater tots on the baking sheet.
- Bake the tots for 25 minutes. Top with the pork and cook for an additional 5 minutes.
- While the tots are cooking toss the cabbage with the, mayonnaise, mustard, and vinegar.
- Top the cooked tots with the BBQ sauce and then the slaw.
- Serve immediately.

Tater Tot Cups with Cheese and Bacon

Prep Time: 10 Min. / **Cook Time:** 30 Min. / **Servings:** 12

Ingredients:
Cooking spray, for pan
2 c. Frozen Tater Tots
1 c. cooked bacon, chopped
1 c. shredded Cheddar
1 c. shredded mozzarella
sour cream, for topping
Sliced green onions, for garnish

Directions:
- Preheat your oven to 350F. Use the cooking spray to coat 12 cup muffin pan.
- Place 3 tots in each muffin cup. Cook for 18 to 20 minutes.
- Take the pan out of the oven and turn on the broiler.
- Once the tots are out of the oven and still warm, coat the bottom of a shot glass with cooking spray. Flatten the tots using the bottom of the shot glass. A well should be created for the other ingredients. Add in the cheese, and bacon.
- Broil for 1 to 2 minutes, just until the cheese melts.
- Allow the cups to cool before topping them with sour cream and green onions.

Alicia Patterson

Cheesy Ranch Bacon Tater Tot Skewers

Prep Time: 10 Min. / **Cook Time:** 35 Min. / **Servings:** 6-8

Ingredients:
1 2-pound bag Tater Tots
8 slices of cooked bacon, chopped
1 cup of cheese, grated
1 tablespoon ranch seasoning

Directions:
- Preheat your oven to 425F. Line a baking sheet with parchment paper.
- Place the tater tots on the baking sheet.
- Bake the tots for about 25 minutes. They should be nice and crispy.
- Let the tots cool for until you can handle them. Put 6 or 7 tots on each skewer.
- Place the skewers back on the baking sheet. Season with ranch seasoning, and top with cheese and bacon.
- Bake for 10 more minutes, until the cheese melts.
- Serve immediately.

Bacon and Cheese Sriracha Tater Tots

Prep Time: 10 Min. / **Cook Time:** 5 Min. / **Servings:** 4

Ingredients:
1 pound frozen Tater Tots, cooked
Nonstick cooking spray
4 slices bacon, cooked and crumbled
1 cup shredded cheddar cheese
1/4 cup sour cream
1/4 cup mayonnaise
2 tablespoons Sriracha
Chopped fresh chives, for topping

Directions:
- Preheat your oven to 400F.
- Pack the tater tots tightly into a baking dish.
- Sprinkle with cheese and bacon.
- Bake the dish for 5 minutes.
- While the tots are baking, use a whisk to combine the mayo, Sriracha, and sour cream.
- Top the cooked tots with the Sriracha mixture and sprinkle with chives.

Alicia Patterson

Bacon and Sausage Nacho Tots

Prep Time: 10 Min. / **Cook Time:** 5 Min. / **Servings:** 8

Ingredients:
2 pounds Tater Tots, cooked
2 cups cheddar cheese shredded
6 slices bacon cooked and crumbled
1/2 cup chorizo or smoked sausage cooked and chopped
1 cup tomatoes diced
4 green onions sliced
1/2 cup sour cream

Directions:
- Preheat your oven to 450F. Line a big rimmed baking sheet with parchment paper.
- Place the tater tots onto the baking sheet.
- Sprinkle with cheese sausage, and bacon.
- Bake the dish for 5 minutes.
- Top the cooked tots with the remaining ingredients and serve.

Tennessee Pulled Pork Barbecue Tater Tot Nachos

Prep Time: 10 Min. / **Cook Time:** 50 Min. / **Servings:** 6

Ingredients:
1, 28-ounce package tater tots
2 cups shredded pepper jack cheese
2 cups cooked pulled pork
1/2 cup chopped white onion
1/4 cup chopped pickled jalapeno peppers
1/2 cup Memphis style barbeque sauce
1 cup prepared coleslaw (optional)
1 bunch green onions, sliced

Directions:
- Preheat your oven to 425F. Line a big rimmed baking sheet with parchment paper.
- Place the tater tots onto the baking sheet.
- Bake the tots for 20 minutes. Then shake the baking sheet and bake for 20 to 25 minutes more. The tots should be golden brown when cooked.
- Turn on your broiler
- Top the cooked tots with the remaining ingredients except for the green onions.
- Place the baking sheet under the broiler for 5 to 7 minutes until the cheese melts.
- Top with the green onions to serve

Pulled Pork Tater Tots with Fontina

Prep Time: 10 Min. / **Cook Time:** 25 Min. / **Servings:** 6

Ingredients:
12 ounces pulled pork
1 (16 ounce) can baked beans
30 - 40 tater tots
2 cups shredded cheddar cheese
1 cup shredded mozzarella
3 green onions, diced
Cooking spray

Directions:
- Preheat your oven to 450F. Coat a 2-quart casserole dish with cooking spray.
- Place the beans in the dish, then the pulled pork, and top with the tots.
- Bake the mixture for 15 minutes.
- Top the mixture with the cheeses and green onions
- Bake for about 10 minutes. The cheese should be melted and the edges should be bubbling when done.
- Serve immediately.

Tater Tots Bacon Cheeseburger Style

Prep Time: 10 Min. / **Cook Time:** 57 Min. / **Servings:** 8

Ingredients:
1 lb. lean (at least 80%) ground beef
1 cup chopped onion
2 teaspoons Montreal steak grill seasoning
1 can (10.5 oz.) condensed cream of onion soup
½ cup sour cream
2 pounds frozen Tater Tots
4 slices cooked bacon, coarsely chopped
2 cups shredded Cheddar cheese
¼ cup chopped green onions

Directions:
- Preheat your oven to 350F. Use cooking spray to coat a 13x9 baking dish.
- Put the onions and beef in a skillet and cook on medium heat for 7 to 9 minutes. Stir the mixture frequently. The mixture is cooked when it turns brown. Drain the oil from the mixture, and mix the meat and onions with the onion soup, Montreal seasoning, and sour cream.
- Put half the tater tots in the baking dish.
- Then add in in the beef mixture and half the cheese and bacon.
- Add the remaining tots and top with the remaining cheese.
- Bake the mixture for 40 minutes and then sprinkle with the rest of the bacon. Cook for another 5 minutes.
- Bake the dish for 5 to 10 more minutes. The edges will be brown and the cheese melted when cooked.
- Top the cooked tots with the green onions and serve.

Cheesy Breakfast Tater Tots with Bacon

Prep Time: 10 Min. / **Cook Time:** 57 Min. / **Servings:** 8

Ingredients:
12 eggs
4 ounces Monterey Jack cheese, shredded (about 1 cup)
1/2 cup whole milk
1/2 teaspoon table salt
1/4 teaspoon black pepper
4 ounces sharp Cheddar cheese, shredded (about 1 cup)
6 thick-cut smoked bacon slices, cooked and crumbled
2 pounds frozen tater tots

Directions:
- Preheat your oven to 350F. Use cooking spray to coat a 13x9 baking dish.
- Put the cheese, milk, eggs, salt and pepper in a big bowl and use a whisk to mix them together.
- Put the tater tots in the baking dish.
- Then add in in the cheese and egg mixture.
- Add the remaining tots and top with the remaining cheese.
- Bake the mixture for 40 to 45 minutes. The eggs should be cooked and the cheese melted when cooked.
- Allow the tots to rest for 10 minutes. Top the cooked tots with the bacon to serve.

Southern Cheesy Bacon Tater Tot Bites

Prep Time: 15 Min. / **Cook Time:** 25 Min. / **Servings:** 8

Ingredients:
2 cups frozen tater tots, at room temperature
1 ounce sharp cheddar cheese, cut into 1/4-inch squares
4 slices bacon, quartered
1/4 cup brown sugar, packed
1 tablespoon chopped fresh parsley leaves

Directions:
- Preheat your oven to 400F. Use parchment to line a baking sheet.
- Place a square of cheese on a tater tot and wrap a piece of bacon around it. Do the same with the remaining, cheese, tots, and bacon.
- Coat all the tots with brown sugar
- Put the tater tots with the bacon seam side on the baking sheet.
- Bake the tots for 20 to 25 minutes. Flip the tots halfway through.
- Top the cooked tots with the parsley to serve.

Alicia Patterson

NOTHIN BUT THE BEEF...& TOTS
Cowboy Tater Tots

Prep Time: 15 Min. / **Cook Time:** 40 Min. / **Servings:** 8-10

Ingredients:

1 lb. ground beef
1/2 onion, chopped
2 garlic cloves, minced
1/2 teaspoon chili powder
1/2 teaspoon cumin
2 cups frozen corn, defrosted
2 cups canned diced tomatoes
1/3 cup sour cream
1 1/2 cups cheese, divided
kosher salt (just enough to taste)
Freshly ground black pepper
2 bags (16 oz.) frozen tater tots
1 tablespoon Chopped parsley, for garnish
1 tablespoon olive oil

Directions:
- Preheat your oven to 375F.
- Put the oil in a big skillet and heat it on medium heat. Add in the onions and cook until they become translucent and soften. Then put in the beef and cook until the beef browns. Drain some of the fat out and move the ingredients to the edge of the skillet. Put in the cumin, garlic, and chili powder and allow everything to cook for around 2 minutes, until the garlic becomes fragrant. Add salt and pepper to taste.
- Pour in the corn, 1 cup of cheese, sour cream, and tomatoes. Allow the mixture to cook, stirring frequently, until the sour cream is mixed in and the cheese melts.
- Put the beef mixture into a 13x9 baking dish.
- Put the tater tots in the baking dish on top of the mixture. Top with the remaining cheese.
- Bake for 20-25, until the tots turn golden and the cheese melts.
- Top with parsley to serve.

Cheeseburger Tater Tot Cups

Prep Time: 10 Min. / **Cook Time:** 30 Min. / **Servings:** 12

Ingredients:

Cooking spray, for pan
36 Frozen Tater Tots
1 pound ground beef
1/2 cup Onion, finely diced
Salt and Pepper to taste
2 tablespoons Mayonnaise
2 tablespoons Yellow mustard
2 tablespoons Ketchup
2 tablespoons Pickle relish
1 cup Cheddar cheese, shredded

Mini Pickles for garnish
Cooking spray

Sauce
1 teaspoon Garlic powder
1/2 cup Mayonnaise
4 tablespoons Pickle relish
2 tablespoons Yellow mustard
1 teaspoon White wine vinegar
1 teaspoon Paprika
1 teaspoon Onion powder

Note: Use more or less of any of these condiments according to your taste!

Directions:

- Preheat your oven to 425F. Use the cooking spray to coat 12 cup muffin pan.
- Put the beef in a skillet and cook it on medium high heat until it browns. Drain the fat from the skillet and add in the onions. Cook the mixture until the onions become soft.
- Mix the beef mixture with the relish, ketchup, mustard, and mayo.
- Place 3 tots in each muffin cup. Cook for 10 minutes.
- Once the tots are out of the oven and still warm, coat the bottom of a shot glass with cooking spray. Flatten the tots using the bottom of the shot glass. A well should be created for the other ingredients. Add in the cheese, and meat mixture.
- Bake for an additional 15 minutes.
- Allow the cups to cool for 5 minutes.
- Mix together all the sauce ingredients while the cups cool.
- Top the cups with the sauce to serve.

Alicia Patterson

Chili Dog Tater Tots

Prep Time: 5 Min. / **Cook Time:** 25 Min. / **Servings:** 8

Ingredients:
1 pound lean ground beef
1 15 oz. can chili beans
1 15 oz. can tomato sauce
4 hot dogs cut into small bites
2 teaspoons chili powder
1/2 teaspoon each garlic powder and onion powder
1/4 teaspoon red pepper flakes optional
1/2 cup chopped onion
3 cups shredded sharp cheddar cheese divided
1 32 oz. pkg. tater tots
Cooking spray

Directions:
- Preheat your oven to 350F. Coat a 9x13 baking dish with cooking spray.
- Put the beef in a skillet and cook it on medium high heat until it browns. Then mix the beef with the hot dogs, beans, chili powder, garlic powder, onion powder, red pepper flakes, and tomato sauce,
- Put the chili in the baking dish, and top with the 2 cups of cheese and onions. Place the tots on top of the cheese.
- Bake the tots for 30 minutes. Then top with the rest of the cheese and cook for 3 to 5 minutes. The cheese should be melted.
- Allow the mixture to cool for a couples before serving.

Philly Cheesesteak Tater Tots

Prep Time: 10 Min. / **Cook Time:** 25 Min. / **Servings:** 8

Ingredients:
1 green pepper, cut into thin strips
1 small onion, cut into thin slices, separated into rings
1/2 lb. thinly shaved roast beef, cut into thin strips
2 VELVEETA Mini Blocks (4 oz. each), cut into 1/2-inch cubes
1 Tablespoon. milk
1, 2-pound bag frozen tater tots
Cooking spray

Directions:
- Preheat your oven to 425F. Use cooking spray to coat a 13x9 baking dish.
- Place the tater tots into the baking dish.
- Bake the tots for about 25 minutes. They should be nice and crispy.
- While the tots are baking put the onions and peppers in a non-stick pan and cook on medium heat for 3 to 5 minutes. Cook until the ingredients become crispy, making sure to stir constantly. Put in the beef, reduce the temperature to medium-low and cook for about 5 minutes, until the beef is hot, stirring throughout.
- Microwave the Velveeta for 2 minutes on high heat, stopping every 30 seconds to stir the cheese.
- Top the cooked tots with the beef mixture and then pour over the Velveeta cheese to serve.

Alicia Patterson

Ground Beef Taco Tater Tots

Prep Time: 5 Min. / **Cook Time:** 25 Min. / **Servings:** 8

Ingredients:

1 pound lean ground beef
1 onion, diced
2 cloves garlic, minced
1 packet taco seasoning mix low sodium
1 cup enchilada sauce, divided
1 1/2 cups frozen corn
1 1/2 cups bell pepper
1 12 oz. can black beans drained and rinsed
3 cups shredded cheddar cheese divided
16 oz. frozen tater tots
1/3 cup salsa

Toppings:
Diced tomatoes
Shredded lettuce
Sour Cream
Avocado Slices

Cooking spray

Directions:

- Preheat your oven to 400F. Coat a 9x13 baking dish with cooking spray.
- Put the beef, onions, and garlic up in a skillet and cook it on medium-high heat until the meat browns. Drain the fat and mix in cup water, corn, bell peppers, 2/3 cup enchilada sauce, and beans. Allow everything to cook for around 5 minutes, until it thickens up.
- Pour the mixture into the baking dish, and top with half the cheese then add the tots. Cook for 30 minutes.
- While the tots are cooking mix together the rest of the enchilada sauce, and salsa.
- Top the tots with the enchilada sauce and remaining cheese. Bake for about 10 more minutes, until the dish is bubbly and the cheese melts.
- Top with the toppings and serve immediately.

Greek Tater Tot Nachos

Prep Time: 10 Min. / **Cook Time:** 25 Min. / **Servings:** 8

Ingredients:
1 pound Lamb Loin Chops, cooked
1 2pound bag Frozen Tater Tots
1/3 cup Kalamata Olives, chopped
1 large Roma Tomato, diced
1/3 cup Roasted Red Pepper, diced
1 Shallot, thinly sliced
1/2 cup Feta Cheese
1 cup Shredded Cheddar Cheese
1/2 cup hummus
Salt and pepper
Cooking spray

Directions:
- Preheat your oven to 425F. Use cooking spray to coat a 13x9 baking dish.
- Place the tater tots into the baking dish and add salt and pepper to taste.
- Bake the tots for about 25 minutes. They should be nice and crispy.
- Top the tots with all the cheddar and half the feta cheese. Bake for another 3 to 5 minutes, until the cheese melts.
- While the tots are finishing, slice the lamb thinly.
- Top the tots with the remaining feta, red pepper, tomatoes, shallots, olives, and hummus.
- Serve immediately.

Tater Tot Beef Dip

Prep Time: 5 Min. / **Cook Time:** 30 Min. / **Servings:** 6-8

Ingredients:
3 cups thawed tater tots
1 cup cooked ground beef
2 teaspoon Mrs. Dash salt-free seasoning or any all-purpose seasoning
2 cups Colby-jack cheese, divided
16 oz. sour cream
1/4 teaspoon salt

Directions:
- Preheat your oven to 375F.
- Chop the tater tots roughly.
- Combine the sour cream, 1 cup cheese, beef, seasoning, and tots in a big bowl.
- Pour the tot mixture into a 9-inch pie pan, and use a spoon to smooth the top. Top with the remaining cheese.
- Bake the mixture for about 30 minutes. The cheese should be bubbling and golden when done.
- Serve the tot dip immediately.

I Love Tater Tots

FOR THE VEGETARIANS

Cheesy Ranch Tater Tots

Prep Time: 5 Min. / **Cook Time:** 20 Min. / **Servings:** 8

Ingredients:
2 pounds Tater Tots
2 cups cheddar cheese shredded
6 slices bacon cooked and crumbled
1/2 cup chorizo or smoked sausage cooked and chopped
1 cup tomatoes diced
4 green onions sliced
1/2 cup sour cream

Directions:
- Preheat your oven to 450F. Use cooking spray to coat a 13x9 baking dish.
- Place the tater tots into the baking dish.
- Bake the tots for about 20 minutes.
- Sprinkle with cheese, and ranch seasoning.
- Cook for an additional 8 minutes until the cheese melts.
- Serve immediately.

Chipotle Tater Tot Nachos

Prep Time: 10 Min. / **Cook Time:** 25 Min. / **Servings:** 8

Ingredients:
1 lb. frozen tater tots
1/3 cup milk
12 slices white American cheese
1 tablespoon. finely chopped chipotles in adobo
3 tablespoons Mexican crema or sour cream thinned with milk
1/3 cup Pico de Gallo
1/3 cup thinly sliced scallions
1/4 cup chopped fresh cilantro
Cooking spray

Directions:
- Preheat your oven to 425F. Use cooking spray to coat a 13x9 baking dish.
- Place the tater tots into the baking dish.
- Bake the tots for about 25 minutes. They should be nice and crispy.
- While the tots are cooking put the chipotles, cheese, and milk in a pan. Cook on medium-low heat, stirring frequently until the mixture becomes smooths. This should take about 8 minutes.
- Top the cooked tots with the cheese mixture then add the rest of the ingredients.
- Serve immediately.

Garlic and Cheese Tater Tot Bundt

Prep Time: 10 Min. / **Cook Time:** 35 Min. / **Servings:** 6-8

Ingredients:
2 tablespoons. butter, melted
1 teaspoon. garlic powder
1/4 c. freshly grated Parmesan
1 c. shredded mozzarella cheese
2 large eggs
3/4 bag frozen tater tots (32 oz.)
Cooking spray

Directions:
- Preheat your oven to 425F. Use cooking spray to coat a Bundt pan.
- Mix all the ingredients except for the tots in a large bowl. Once well mixed, toss the tots in the mixture until well coated.
- Place the tots and seasoning mixture in the Bundt pan and pack the tots tightly in the pan.
- Bake the tots for 30 to 35 minutes until they're golden.
- Let the tots cool for about 10 minutes before remove them from the pan.

Rosemary Tater Tot with Malt Vinegar Dipping Sauce

Prep Time: 10 Min. / **Cook Time:** 25 Min. / **Servings:** 6-8

Ingredients:
1 2-pound bag Tater Tots
3 sprigs fresh rosemary, stemmed and chopped
1/2 teaspoon flaky sea salt

Sauce:
1/2 cup sour cream
2 teaspoons Dijon mustard
2 teaspoons malt vinegar
Sea salt and freshly ground black pepper

Directions:
- Preheat your oven to 425F. Use cooking spray to coat a 13x9 baking dish.
- Place the tater tots into the baking dish.
- Bake the tots for about 25 minutes. They should be nice and crispy.
- While the tots are cooking mix all the sauce ingredients together.
- Mix the cooked tots with the salt and rosemary.
- Serve the cooked tots with the vinegar sauce.

Asian BBQ Tater Tots

Prep Time: 10 Min. / **Cook Time:** 25 Min. / **Servings:** 6-8

Ingredients:
1 2-pound bag Tater Tots
3/4 cups hoisin sauce
1/4 cup Asian chili sauce
1/4 cup unseasoned rice vinegar
1/4 cup chicken stock
2 tablespoons fresh ginger
1 teaspoon toasted sesame oil
2 tablespoons toasted sesame seeds
2 tablespoons green onions, sliced thinly, garnish
salt and pepper to taste

Directions:
- Preheat your oven to 425F. Use cooking spray to coat a 13x9 baking dish.
- Place the tater tots into the baking dish.
- Bake the tots for about 25 minutes. They should be nice and crispy.
- While the tots are cooking, place everything buy the green onions, and the sesame seeds in a saucepan and bring to a light simmer. Stir the mixture, and allow it to cook for 5 to 7 minutes, until it thickens
- Toss the tots with the sauce and top with the green onions and sesame seeds.

Parmesan Tater Tots

Prep Time: 5 Min. / **Cook Time:** 25 Min. / **Servings:** 6-8

Ingredients:
1, 2-pound bag tater tots
2 tablespoons olive oil
2 teaspoons Italian seasoning
1 1/2 tablespoons crushed garlic
1/2 cup grated parmesan
salt and pepper
nonstick cooking spray

Directions:
- Preheat your oven to 425F. Use cooking spray to coat a baking sheet.
- Place the tots in a bowl and toss with the salt and pepper, Italian seasoning, and olive oil.
- Place the tater tots on the baking sheets.
- Bake the tots for 15 to 20 minutes. They should be nice and crispy.
- Put the tots in a bowl and toss them with the parmesan and garlic
- Serve the cooked tots immediately.

Cheesy Buffalo Tater Tots

Prep Time: 10 Min. / **Cook Time:** 35 Min. / **Servings:** 8

Ingredients:
32 oz. frozen tater tots
1/2 cup buffalo sauce
1 cup shredded cheddar cheese
4 oz. blue cheese crumbles
Cooking spray

Directions:
- Preheat your oven to 425F. Use cooking spray to lightly coat a rimmed baking sheet.
- Place the tater tots on the baking sheet.
- Bake the tots for about 28 to 30 minutes. They should be extra crispy.
- Mix the tots with the buffalo sauce and place them back on the baking sheet.
- Top the tots with both cheeses and bake until the cheese is melty, about 5 minutes.
- Serve immediately.

Thyme Tater Tot with Ranch Dressing

Prep Time: 5 Min. / **Cook Time:** 25 Min. / **Servings:** 6-8

Ingredients:
1 2-pound bag Tater Tots
3 sprigs fresh thyme, stemmed and chopped
1/2 teaspoon flaky sea salt
1 cup ranch dressing

Directions:
- Preheat your oven to 425F. Use cooking spray to coat a 13x9 baking dish.
- Place the tater tots into the baking dish.
- Bake the tots for about 25 minutes. They should be nice and crispy.
- Mix the cooked tots with the salt and thyme.
- Serve the cooked tots with the ranch dressing.

Cajun Tater Tots

Prep Time: 5 Min. / **Cook Time:** 25 Min. / **Servings:** 6-8

Ingredients:
1, 2-pound bag Tater Tots
4 teaspoons no salt added Cajun seasoning
1/2 teaspoon flaky sea salt
¼ teaspoon cayenne (optional)
1 cup ranch dressing

Directions:
- Preheat your oven to 425F. Use cooking spray to coat a 13x9 baking dish.
- Place the tots in a bowl and toss with the salt and Cajun seasoning.
- Place the tater tots into the baking dish.
- Bake the tots for about 25 minutes. They should be nice and crispy.
- Serve the cooked tots immediately.

Alicia Patterson

Old Bay Tater Tots

Prep Time: 5 Min. / **Cook Time:** 25 Min. / **Servings:** 6-8

Ingredients:
1, 2-pound bag Tater Tots
1 tablespoon Old Bay seasoning

Directions:
- Preheat your oven to 425F. Use cooking spray to coat a 13x9 baking dish.
- Place the tots in a bowl and toss with the Old Bay seasoning.
- Place the tater tots into the baking dish.
- Bake the tots for about 25 minutes. They should be nice and crispy.
- Serve the cooked tots immediately.

Taco Flavored Tater Tots

Prep Time: 5 Min. / **Cook Time:** 25 Min. / **Servings:** 6-8

Ingredients:
1, 2-pound bag Tater Tots
1 package taco seasoning

Directions:
- Preheat your oven to 425F. Use cooking spray to coat a 13x9 baking dish.
- Place the tots in a bowl and toss with the taco seasoning.
- Place the tater tots into the baking dish.
- Bake the tots for about 25 minutes. They should be nice and crispy.
- Serve the cooked tots immediately.

Smokey Paprika Tater Tots with Chipotle Ketchup

Prep Time: 5 Min. / **Cook Time:** 25 Min. / **Servings:** 6-8

Ingredients:
1, 2-pound bag Tater Tots
2 teaspoons smoked sweet paprika
1 1/2 cups organic ketchup
1 tablespoon chipotle in adobo sauce, seeded and pureed

Directions:
- Preheat your oven to 425F. Use cooking spray to coat a 13x9 baking dish.
- Place the tots in a bowl and toss with the paprika.
- Place the tater tots into the baking dish.
- Bake the tots for about 25 minutes. They should be nice and crispy.
- While the tots are baking mix the ketchup and chipotle until well combined.
- Serve the cooked tots immediately with the chipotle ketchup.

Buffalo Ranch Tater Tots

Prep Time: 5 Min. / **Cook Time:** 25 Min. / **Servings:** 8

Ingredients:
1 bag of frozen tater tots
1/3 cup buffalo sauce
1 packet of ranch seasoning
Blue cheese, for garnish

Directions:
- Preheat your oven to 450F. Line a baking sheet with parchment paper.
- Mix the buffalo sauce, ranch seasoning, and tater tots together in a bowl.
- Put the tater tots on the baking sheet.
- Bake the tots for 20 to 25 minutes. Until crunchy and cooked through
- Garnish with the blue cheeses to serve.

Feta Tater Tots

Prep Time: 5 Min. / **Cook Time:** 25 Min. / **Servings:** 8

Ingredients:
1 2-pound bag of frozen tater tots
¾ cup feta cheese
Red chili flakes
Salt and pepper
Parsley for garnish

Directions:
- Preheat your oven to 450F. Line a baking sheet with parchment paper.
- Toss the tater tots with the red chili flakes, salt, and pepper to taste together in a bowl.
- Put the tater tots on the baking sheet.
- Bake the tots for 20 minutes. Top with the feta and bake for 5 more minutes.
- Garnish with the parsley to serve.

Italian Seasoned Tater Tots

Prep Time: 5 Min. / **Cook Time:** 25 Min. / **Servings:** 6-8

Ingredients:
1, 2-pound bag tater tots
2 tablespoons olive oil
2 teaspoons garlic powder
2 teaspoons chili powder
2 teaspoons Italian seasoning
salt and pepper
nonstick cooking spray

Directions:
- Preheat your oven to 425F. Use cooking spray to coat a baking sheet.
- Place the tots in a bowl and toss with all the other ingredients.
- Place the tater tots on the baking sheets.
- Bake the tots for 15 to 20 minutes. They should be nice and crispy.
- Serve the cooked tots immediately.

Alicia Patterson

Jalapeno Popper Tater Tots

Prep Time: 10 Min. / **Cook Time:** 35 Min. / **Servings:** 6-8

Ingredients:
2, 8 oz. packages of cream cheese, softened at room temperature.
1 cup sour cream
2 cups Mexican Cheddar Jack Shredded Cheese, divided
1 pound bacon, cooked and crumbled
6 Jalapeno Peppers, deseeded and diced
1, 2 lb. bag of tater tots
6 green onions, thinly sliced
Cooking spray

Directions:
- Preheat your oven to 425F. Use cooking spray to coat a casserole dish.
- Place the tater tots into the casserole dish.
- Bake the tots for about 15 minutes.
- While the tots are cooking, mix together the sour cream, jalapenos, cream cheese, most of the bacon, 1   cups cheddar cheese, and most of the green onions.
- Pour and spread the cheese mixture over the tater tots. Top with the remaining, cheese, green onions, and bacon.
- Cook the mixture for another 20 minutes.
- Serve the cooked tots immediately.

Korean Ginger and Garlic Tater Tots with Spicy Cheese Sauce

Prep Time: 5 Min. / **Cook Time:** 25 Min. / **Servings:** 6-8

Ingredients:
1 pound frozen tater tots
½ teaspoon onion powder
½ teaspoon garlic powder
½ teaspoon ground ginger
¼ teaspoon salt
8 oz. shredded sharp cheddar cheese
1 tablespoon cornstarch
1, 12 oz. can of evaporated milk
1-2 tablespoons gochujang

Directions:
- Preheat your oven to 425F. Use cooking spray to coat a baking sheet.
- Combine the salt, garlic and onion powder, and ginger in a large bowl. Toss the tots in the mixture until well coated.
- Place the tater tots on the baking sheets.
- Bake the tots for 15 to 20 minutes. They should be nice and crispy.
- While the tots are baking, put the cheese and cornstarch in a pan. Then pour in the evaporated milk and gochujang. Heat the mixture on low heat, until the cheese melts, and the sauce becomes thicker. Make sure you stir the mixture frequently.
- Serve the cooked tots with a side of the sauce.

CHICKEN

Chicken Tater Tot Casserole

Prep Time: 5 Min. / **Cook Time:** 45 Min. / **Servings:** 5

Ingredients:
1/4 cup 2% low-fat milk
1 cup low-fat sour cream
1, 10-ounce can of condensed cream of chicken soup
2 boneless skinless chicken breasts, cooked & cubed
16 ounces frozen tater tots
1 1/2 cups of shredded Colby or Monterey jack cheese

Directions:
- Preheat your oven to 350F.
- Mix all the ingredients in a bowl until well combined
- Pour the mixture into a 12x9 baking dish.
- Bake the mixture for about 45 minutes.
- Serve immediately.

Ranch Cheesy Chicken Tater Tot Casserole

Prep Time: 5 Min. / **Cook Time:** 45 Min. / **Servings:** 6-8

Ingredients:
3 cups chopped cooked chicken
16-oz sour cream
1 can Cream of Chicken soup
1, 1 oz. package Original Ranch dressing mix
1, 3 oz. bag real bacon pieces
2 cups shredded cheddar cheese
2 lb. bag frozen tater tots
Cooking spray

Directions:
- Preheat your oven to 350F. Coat a 9x13 baking dish with cooking spray.
- Mix all the ingredients except the tots in a big bowl. Then mix in the tots.
- Pour the mixture into the baking dish.
- Cook the mixture for 40 to 45 minutes. It will be bubbling when cooked.
- Serve immediately.

Alicia Patterson

Double Cheesy Chicken Tater Tot Casserole

Prep Time: 5 Min. / **Cook Time:** 45 Min. / **Servings:** 6-8

Ingredients:
1 Cup Sour Cream
2 Cans Condensed Cheddar Cheese Soup
1/3 Cup Milk
1 Cup Shredded Cheddar Cheese
1/2 Teaspoon Salt
1 Teaspoon Pepper
1 Teaspoon Garlic Powder
1 Packet Ranch Seasoning Mix
3 Cups Cooked shredded chicken
1/2 cup shredded cheddar cheese
32 Ounce Package Frozen Tater Tots
Cooking spray

Directions:
- Preheat your oven to 350F. Lightly coat a 9x13 baking dish with cooking spray.
- Mix the first 8 ingredients in a big bowl. Then mix in the chicken and finally the tots.
- Pour the cheese mixture into the baking dish. Cover the dish with aluminum foil.
- Cook the mixture for 30 minutes. It will be bubbling when cooked.
- Take off the aluminum foil and top with the c up of cheddar cheese. Bake for an additional 10 to 15 minutes. The cheese will be melted when finished.
- Serve immediately.

Buffalo Chicken Tater Tot Skillet

Prep Time: 10 Min. / **Cook Time:** 30 Min. / **Servings:** 4

Ingredients:
1 8-ounce package Cream Cheese
1/2 cup Frank's Red-Hot Sauce
1 packet Ranch Seasoning, Divided
1 1/2 cups Cooked Chicken, Diced
12 ounces Frozen Mixed Vegetables
1/4 cup Shredded Cheddar Cheese
1 pound package Frozen Tater Tots

Directions:
- Preheat your oven to 425F.
- Heat a 12-inch cast iron skillet on medium heat. Put in the hot sauce, 2 tablespoons ranch seasoning, and cream cheese.
- Pour the cheese mixture into the baking dish. Cover the dish with aluminum foil. Stir the mixture until it melts. Remove the skillet from the heat and mix in the vegetable and chicken.
- Make sure the contents are well spread throughout the skillet. Top with cheese.
- Place the tots on top of the cheese in a single layer. Season with the remaining ranch seasoning.
- Cook the mixture for about 25 minutes. That tots will be crispy when cooked.
- Serve immediately.

Alicia Patterson

Chicken and Stuffing Tater Tot Casserole

Prep Time: 10 Min. / **Cook Time:** 45 Min. / **Servings:** 10

Ingredients:
olive oil cooking spray
4 skinless, boneless chicken strips
1 (10.5 ounce) can chicken gravy
1 (10.5 ounce) can cream of chicken soup
1 cup evaporated milk
1 cup sage and onion stuffing mix
1/2 cup minced onion
2 teaspoons minced garlic
1/4 teaspoon celery seed
ground black pepper to taste
1, 32-ounce package frozen tater tots
1/2 cup shredded mozzarella cheese
1/2 cup shredded Cheddar cheese

Directions:
- Preheat your oven to 375F. Coat a 13x9 baking dish with the cooking spray.
- Coat a large skillet with cooking spray and heat it on medium heat. Put in the chicken and cook for about 4 minutes per side, until the juices are clear.
- Slice the chicken into cubes, and put it in a big bowl along with the milk, gravy, stuffing, soup, celery seed, onions, and black pepper. Mix until all ingredients are well combined.
- Put the tots in the baking dish. Pour in the soup mixture, and top with the cheese.
- Cook the mixture for about 45 minutes. The mixture should be golden and bubbling when cooked.
- Serve immediately.

Mexican Chicken and Tater Tot Casserole

Prep Time: 15 Min. / **Cook Time:** 27 Min. / **Servings:** 6

Ingredients:
3 cups cooked, diced chicken
1, 10-ounce can hot diced tomatoes & chilies, drained
1, 10.5 ounce can cream of chicken soup
2 green onions, diced
16 ounces frozen tater tot potatoes
2 cups Mexican blend cheese
Cilantro
Cooking spray

Directions:
- Preheat your oven to 350F. Coat an 11x8 baking dish with cooking spray.
- Mix together the first 4 ingredients in a large bowl.
- Pour the mixture into the baking dish. Top with the tots and sprinkle the cheese on the tots.
- Bake the mixture for 25 minutes. Then turn on the broiler.
- Broil the mixture for no more than 2 minutes. You just want to brown the cheese, so watch it closely.
- Serve immediately.

Alicia Patterson

Chicken Tender and Cheese Tater Tot Casserole

Prep Time: 10 Min. / **Cook Time:** 45 Min. / **Servings:** 8

Ingredients:
16 ounces sour cream
1 package ranch dressing mix
4 cups cheddar cheese, divided
1 lb. chicken tenders, chopped in bite size pieces
1 can cream of chicken soup
2 pounds frozen tater tots

Cooking spray

Directions:
- Preheat your oven to 350F. Coat a 9x13 baking dish with cooking spray.
- Mix together half the cheese, ranch dressing, sour cream and soup in a large bowl. Then mix in the chicken and finally the tots.
- Pour the mixture into the baking dish.
- Bake the mixture for 40 minutes. Then top with the remaining cheese and bake for 5 more minutes.
- Serve immediately.

Chicken Pot Pie Tater Tot Casserole

Prep Time: 10 Min. / **Cook Time:** 45 Min. / **Servings:** 6

Ingredients:
1 Tablespoon. butter
1 pkg. (16 oz.) frozen vegetable blend
1/2 cup chopped onions
2 cups chopped cooked chicken
1 can 10 3/4 oz. condensed cream of chicken soup
1/4 cup milk
1 Tablespoon. chopped fresh thyme
1 pound frozen tater tots
Cooking spray

Directions:
- Preheat your oven to 375F. Coat an 11x7 baking dish with cooking spray.
- Place the butter in a big skillet and melt it on medium heat. Put in the onions and vegetables and allow them to cook for 3 minutes, stirring throughout. Stir in the thyme, soup, chicken, and milk and allow the mixture to cook for 3 more minutes. Stir the mixture throughout.
- Pour the mixture into the baking dish. Then top with the tots.
- Bake the mixture for 45 minutes. The dish is done when the tots are golden, and everything else is hot.
- Serve immediately.

Chicken Broccoli Cheddar Tater Tot Casserole

Prep Time: 10 Min. / **Cook Time:** 50 Min. / **Servings:** 6

Ingredients:
2 pounds frozen tater tots
1 can cream of chicken soup
1 can cheddar cheese soup
1 bag (16 ounce) frozen broccoli
1 pound chicken, cubed
½ cup cheddar cheese
10.75-ounce water
Cooking spray

Directions:
- Preheat your oven to 350F. Coat a 9x13 baking dish with cooking spray.
- Put both of the soups and the water in a saucepan and heat on medium heat until hot. Then add in the broccoli.
- Place as many tots as you can fit in the baking dish
- Pour the mixture into the baking dish along with the chicken. Then top with the remaining tots and cheddar.
- Bake the mixture for 50 minutes. The dish is done when the tots are golden, and the chicken is cooked.
- Serve immediately.

I Love Tater Tots

Chicken Fajita Breakfast Tater Tot Casserole

Prep Time: 10 Min. / **Cook Time:** 50 Min. / **Servings:** 8-10

Ingredients:
1¼ cup milk
1 teaspoon fresh cracked pepper
½ teaspoon onion powder
½ teaspoon garlic powder
½ cup heavy cream
3 large eggs
1½ teaspoon kosher salt
2 large grilled chicken breast, thinly sliced or cubed to ¼ inch pieces
1 cup diced red bell pepper, about 1 large pepper
1 cup diced green bell pepper, about 1 large pepper
2 cups sharp cheddar cheese
1 cup pepper jack cheese
2 pounds frozen tater tots
¼ finely chopped green onions
cilantro and sour cream
Cooking spray

Directions:
- Preheat your oven to 350F. Coat a 9x13 baking dish with cooking spray.
- Combine the milk, pepper, onion and garlic powder, cream, eggs, and salt in a large bowl using a whisk.
- Pour the mixture into the baking dish. Then add in the chicken, then the bell peppers, and top with 1 c ups of cheddar, and the pepper jack and then finally the tots.
- Bake the mixture for 35 to 40 minutes until the cheese sets, and the tots turn golden. Top the mixture with the rest of the cheddar and bake for 8 to 10 more minutes, until the cheese starts to turn golden brown.
- Serve immediately with a garnish of green onions and a side of cilantro and sour cream.

Southwestern Tater Tot Casserole

Prep Time: 10 Min. / **Cook Time:** 40 Min. / **Servings:** 8

Ingredients:
2 pounds Tater Tots
1 pound Boneless Skinless Chicken Breast, into cubes or strips
2 1/4 ounces Ripe Olives Drained, sliced
14 ounces Corn Drained
1 cup Salsa
1 cup Ranch Dressing
1 Onion Chopped
1 1/2 tablespoons garlic Powder
2 teaspoons McCormick Hot Shot Seasoning
2 cups Cheddar Cheese Shredded
Sour Cream
Cooking spray

Directions:
- Preheat your oven to 350F. Coat a 19x13 baking dish with cooking spray.
- Mix everything but the sour cream and cheese in a large bowl.
- Pour the mixture into the baking dish.
- Bake the mixture for 30 minutes. Then top with the cheddar and bake for 5 to 10 more minutes, until the cheese melts.
- Serve immediately with a garnish of sour cream.

SWEET POTATO TOTS

Sweet Potato Tater Tot Casserole

Prep Time: 10 Min. / **Cook Time:** 35 Min. / **Servings:** 8

Ingredients:
2 bags sweet Potato tater tots
1 can of 98% fat-free cream of mushroom soup
1 bag of frozen vegetables
1 lb. of 93% fat-free ground beef.
2 cups of cheddar cheese
Cooking spray

Directions:
- Preheat your oven to 350F. Coat a 2-quart casserole dish with cooking spray.
- Put the beef in a skillet and cook it on medium-high heat until the meat browns. Drain the fat.
- Place the beef, soup, and vegetables in the casserole dish. Top with the tots.
- Bake the mixture for 25 minutes. Top the casserole with the cheese and bake for 10 more minutes.
- Serve immediately.

Sweet Potato Tater Tot Nachos

Prep Time: 15 Min. / **Cook Time:** 33 Min. / **Servings:** 8

Ingredients:
1 20-ounce bag frozen sweet potato tots
1 medium tomato, chopped
1 jalapeño pepper, minced
2 tablespoons lime juice
2 tablespoons chopped fresh cilantro, plus more for garnish
¼ teaspoon salt
¼ cup sour cream
2 tablespoons water
½ teaspoon chili powder
1 cup rinsed, drained reduced-sodium black beans
1 cup shredded Mexican cheese blend
1 medium avocado, chopped
1 cup shredded iceberg or romaine lettuce

Directions:
- Preheat your oven to 425F.
- Place the tots in a single layer in a cast iron skillet. Bake them for 30 minutes, stirring halfway through.
- While the tots are cooking, mix the salt, lime juice, jalapeno, cilantro and tomatoes in a bowl. In a separate bowl mix the chili powder, sour cream, and water.
- Move the tots to the middle of the skillet. Place the cheese and beans on top and bake for an additional 2 to 3 minutes. The cheese should be melted when done.
- Top with the tomato mixture, then lettuce and avocado, and finally the sour cream mixture and cilantro
- Serve immediately.

Rosemary Thyme and Sea Salt Sweet Potato Tater Tots

0Prep Time: 5 Min. / **Cook Time:** 27 Min. / **Servings:** 8-10

Ingredients:
2 bags sweet potato tater tots
2 sprigs fresh rosemary, stemmed and chopped
2 sprigs fresh thyme, stemmed and chopped
3/4 teaspoon flaky sea salt
Cooking spray

Directions:
- Preheat your oven to 425F. Use cooking spray to coat a 13x9 baking dish.
- Toss the tots with the salt, thyme and rosemary in a bowl
- Place the tater tots into the baking dish.
- Bake the tots for about 27 minutes. They should be nice and crispy.
- Serve immediately.

Paprika and Thyme Sweet Potato Tater Tots

Prep Time: 5 Min. / **Cook Time:** 27 Min. / **Servings:** 8-10

Ingredients:
2 bags sweet potato tater tots
2 teaspoons paprika
2 sprigs fresh thyme, stemmed and chopped
1/4 teaspoon flaky sea salt
Cooking spray

Directions:
- Preheat your oven to 425F. Use cooking spray to coat a 13x9 baking dish.
- Toss the tots with the salt, thyme and paprika in a bowl.
- Place the tater tots into the baking dish.
- Bake the tots for about 27 minutes. They should be nice and crispy.
- Serve immediately.

Sweet and Spicy Sweet Potato Tater Tots

Prep Time: 5 Min. / **Cook Time:** 27 Min. / **Servings:** 8-10

Ingredients:
 2 bags sweet potato tater tots
 1 tablespoon brown sugar
 salt and pepper
 1/2 teaspoon cayenne pepper
 Cooking spray

Directions:
- Preheat your oven to 425F. Use cooking spray to coat a 13x9 baking dish.
- Toss the tots with the brown sugar, cayenne, and salt and pepper to taste in a bowl.
- Place the tater tots into the baking dish.
- Bake the tots for about 27 minutes. They should be nice and crispy.
- Serve immediately.

Cajun Spiced Sweet Potato Tater Tots

Prep Time: 5 Min. / **Cook Time:** 27 Min. / **Servings:** 8-10

Ingredients:
2 bags sweet potato tater tots
1 teaspoon sea salt
3 teaspoons garlic powder
3 teaspoons smoked paprika
3 teaspoons dried oregano
2 teaspoons dried thyme
½ teaspoon black pepper
½ teaspoon cayenne pepper
Cooking spray

Directions:
- Preheat your oven to 425F. Use cooking spray to coat a 13x9 baking dish.
- Toss the tots with all the seasoning in a bowl.
- Place the tater tots into the baking dish.
- Bake the tots for about 27 minutes. They should be nice and crispy.
- Serve immediately.

Cumin Chili Powder and Garlic Sweet Potato Tater Tots

Prep Time: 5 Min. / **Cook Time:** 27 Min. / **Servings:** 8-10

Ingredients:
2 bags sweet potato tater tots
1/2 teaspoon chili powder
1/2 teaspoon Garlic powder
1/2 teaspoon ground cumin
1/2 teaspoon sea salt
Cooking spray

Directions:
- Preheat your oven to 425F. Use cooking spray to coat a 13x9 baking dish.
- Toss the tots with all the seasoning in a bowl.
- Place the tater tots into the baking dish.
- Bake the tots for about 27 minutes. They should be nice and crispy.
- Serve immediately.

Alicia Patterson

Moroccan Spiced Sweet Potato Tater Tots

Prep Time: 5 Min. / **Cook Time:** 27 Min. / **Servings:** 8-10

Ingredients:
2 bags sweet potato tater tots
1/2 Tablespoon ground cumin
1 teaspoon ground turmeric
1 teaspoon cinnamon
1/4 teaspoon cayenne pepper
1 teaspoon paprika
1/4 teaspoon salt
Cooking spray

Directions:
- Preheat your oven to 425F. Use cooking spray to coat a 13x9 baking dish.
- Toss the tots with all the seasoning in a bowl.
- Place the tater tots into the baking dish.
- Bake the tots for about 27 minutes. They should be nice and crispy.
- Serve immediately.

Za'atar Sweet Potato Tater Tots with Tahini Dip Sauce

Prep Time: 10 Min. / **Cook Time:** 27 Min. / **Servings:** 8-10

Ingredients:
2 bags sweet potato tater tots
2 teaspoons Za'atar
salt and pepper

Tahini Sauce:
½ cup tahini
¼ teaspoon sea salt
¼ teaspoon garlic powder
¼ cup warm water
Cooking spray

Directions:
- Preheat your oven to 425F. Use cooking spray to coat a 13x9 baking dish.
- Toss the tots with the Za'atar and salt and pepper to taste in a bowl.
- Place the tater tots into the baking dish.
- Bake the tots for about 27 minutes. They should be nice and crispy.
- While the tots are baking, use a whisk to combine the tahini, garlic powder, and sea salt in a bowl. Slowly whisk in the water until your desired consistency is reached.
- Serve immediately with the tahini sauce.

Alicia Patterson

Herbs De Provence Sweet Potato Tater Tots

Prep Time: 5 Min. / **Cook Time:** 27 Min. / **Servings:** 8-10

Ingredients:
2 bags sweet potato tater tots
2 teaspoons herbs de Provence
salt and pepper

Directions:
- Preheat your oven to 425F. Use cooking spray to coat a 13x9 baking dish.
- Toss the tots with the herbs de Provence and salt and pepper to taste in a bowl.
- Place the tater tots into the baking dish.
- Bake the tots for about 27 minutes. They should be nice and crispy.
- Serve immediately.

Indian Spiced Sweet Potato Tater Tots

Prep Time: 5 Min. / **Cook Time:** 27 Min. / **Servings:** 8-10

Ingredients:
2 bags sweet potato tater tots
1/2 teaspoon coriander seeds
1/2 teaspoon cumin seeds
1/2 teaspoon brown or black mustard seeds
1/2 teaspoon turmeric
4 fresh curry leaves, optional
2 tablespoons chopped fresh cilantro
Juice of 1/2 lime

Directions:
- Preheat your oven to 425F. Use cooking spray to coat a 13x9 baking dish.
- Toss the tots with all the herbs and spices except for the cilantro and add salt and pepper to taste in a bowl.
- Place the tater tots into the baking dish.
- Bake the tots for about 27 minutes. They should be nice and crispy.
- Top the cook tots with the lime juice and garnish with cilantro to serve.

Greek Inspired Sweet Potato Tater Tots

Prep Time: 5 Min. / **Cook Time:** 27 Min. / **Servings:** 8-10

Ingredients:
2 bags sweet potato tater tots
2 ½ tablespoons freshly chopped parsley
Juice of half a lemon
2 teaspoon cumin
salt and pepper to taste

Directions:
- Preheat your oven to 425F. Use cooking spray to coat a 13x9 baking dish.
- Toss the tots with the cumin and salt and pepper to taste in a bowl.
- Place the tater tots into the baking dish.
- Bake the tots for about 27 minutes. They should be nice and crispy.
- Toss the cooked tots with the lemon juice and the parsley.
- Serve immediately.

Dijon Sweet Potato Tater Tots

Prep Time: 5 Min. / **Cook Time:** 27 Min. / **Servings:** 8-10

Ingredients:
2 bags sweet potato tater tots
½ cup Dijon mustard
1 ¾ Tablespoon. maple syrup
1 ¾ teaspoon. fresh thyme leaves
salt and pepper to taste
cooking spray

Directions:
- Preheat your oven to 425F. Use cooking spray to coat a 13x9 baking dish and line it with parchment paper.
- Toss the tots with all the other ingredients in a bowl.
- Place the tater tots into the baking dish.
- Bake the tots for about 27 minutes. They should be nice and crispy.
- Serve immediately.

Spanish Spiced Sweet Potato Tater Tots

Prep Time: 5 Min. / **Cook Time:** 27 Min. / **Servings:** 8-10

Ingredients:
2 bags sweet potato tater tots
12 fresh sage leaves
3/4 teaspoon sea salt
1/2 teaspoon smoked paprika
2 teaspoons sherry vinegar
1 teaspoon honey

Directions:
- Preheat your oven to 425F. Use cooking spray to coat a 13x9 baking dish.
- Toss the tots with sage leaves and salt in a bowl.
- Place the tater tots into the baking dish.
- Bake the tots for about 27 minutes. They should be nice and crispy.
- Toss the cooked tots with the paprika, honey and sherry vinegar to serve.

Mexican Inspired Sweet Potato Tater Tots

Prep Time: 5 Min. / **Cook Time:** 27 Min. / **Servings:** 8-10

Ingredients:
2 bags sweet potato tater tots
2 teaspoons cumin
2 teaspoons smoked paprika
1 teaspoon chili flakes
1 teaspoon salt
1 teaspoon garlic powder
3 tablespoons olive oil
Juice of 1 lime

Directions:
- Preheat your oven to 425F. Use cooking spray to coat a 13x9 baking dish.
- Toss the tots with all the ingredients in a bowl.
- Place the tater tots into the baking dish.
- Bake the tots for about 27 minutes. They should be nice and crispy.
- Serve immediately.

Alicia Patterson

TATER TOTS FOR DESSERT
Churro Tater Tots with Dulce De Leche Sauce

Prep Time: 2 Hours 10 Min. / **Cook Time:** 20 Min. / **Servings:** 8-10

Ingredients:
1 can sweetened condensed milk
1/2 cup sugar
2 1/2 tablespoons cinnamon
1 package frozen plain tater tots
peanut oil or canola oil for frying
Flaky sea salt

Directions:
- Remove the paper label for the milk can put the can in a deep pot. Fill the pot with enough water so that there's 2 inches of water above the can. Bring to a boil and then low heat to medium-low and allow the can to cook for at least 2 hours. Check on the pot throughout and add more water when necessary.
- Towards the end of the cooking process, attach a thermometer to a deep pot and fill about halfway with oil. Bring the oil to 375F. Preheat your oven to 200F. Combine the cinnamon and sugar in a bowl. Place a wire rack on a baking sheet
- Fry the tots in batches for 3 to 4 minutes until golden brown. Immediately coat the tots with the cinnamon mixture. Then place them on the wire rack. Place the baking sheet with wire rack in the oven between batches to keep the cooked tots warm.
- Open the can of condensed milk and place it in a bowl. Top with a little sea salt.
- Serve the tots with the dulce de leche sauce.

Apple Tater Tot Crisp

Prep Time: 20 Min. / **Cook Time:** 35 Min. / **Servings:** 8

Ingredients:
1, 2-pound bag tater tots
1 1/2 cups white cheddar cheese, shredded

Apple Filling:
2 large granny smith apples, peeled, core removed, sliced
2/3 cup granulated sugar
1/2 teaspoon ground nutmeg
1 tablespoon fresh lemon juice
1 tablespoon all-purpose flour
2 tablespoons unsalted butter, room temperature

granola topping:
1/4 cup all-purpose flour
2 1/2 tablespoons brown sugar
1/4 teaspoon ground cinnamon
1/4 teaspoon kosher salt
2 tablespoons unsalted butter, room temperature
1/2 cup plain granola

Directions:
- Preheat your oven to 425F.
- Mix all the apple filling ingredients in a bowl until well combined.
- Mix all the ingredients for the granola topping except for the butter in a bowl. Use your hands to mix the butter in with the rest of the ingredients.
- Place the tots in a single layer in a cast iron skillet. Top with the apple mixture and then the granola mixture. Bake for around 25 to 30 minutes.
- Top the mixture with the cheese and bake for 5 more minutes.
- Serve immediately.

Chocolate Covered Bacon Wrapped Tater Tots

Prep Time: 15 Min. / **Cook Time:** 25 Min. / **Servings:** 8-10

Ingredients:
35 frozen tater tots
1 pound gourmet bacon
1 bag semi-sweet chocolate chips
Toothpicks, soaked in water
Cooking spray

Directions:
- Preheat your oven to 425F. Use cooking spray to coat a baking sheet.
- Cut the bacon into thirds. Wrapped the bacon around the tater tots and use a toothpick to secure them.
- Place the tater tots on the baking sheet.
- Bake the tots for about 20 to 25 minutes. They should be golden brown and the bacon cooked through. Take the toothpicks out of the cooked tots.
- Line another baking sheet with parchment paper. Put 1 inch of water in a small pot and bring it to a boil on high heat. Pour the chocolate into a medium sized heat-proof bowl.
- Once the water is boiling, turn off the heat and place the bowl of chocolate on top. Stir the chocolate frequently until it's completely melted.
- Coat the tots with the chocolate and place them on the parchment paper lined baking sheet
- Put the baking sheet in the refrigerator for around 5 minutes until the chocolate cools and hardens.

Cinnamon Sugar Sweet Potato Tater Tots

Prep Time: 5 Min. / **Cook Time:** 27 Min. / **Servings:** 8-10

Ingredients:
1 pound sweet potato tater tots
1/2 - 1 Tablespoon sugar
1/2 teaspoon ground cinnamon
1/4 teaspoon salt
2 tablespoons coconut flour
1/2 teaspoon cinnamon
1/4 cup almond meal

Directions:
- Preheat your oven to 425F. Use cooking spray to coat a 13x9 baking dish.
- Mix all the ingredients but the tots together in a bowl
- Coat the tots with the sugar.
- Place the tater tots into the baking dish.
- Bake the tots for about 27 minutes. They should be nice and crispy.
- Serve immediately.

Alicia Patterson

Tater Tots with Chocolate Peppermint Icing and Crushed Candy Canes

Prep Time: 5 Min. / **Cook Time:** 25 Min. / **Servings:** 8-10

Ingredients:
1, 2-pound bag tater tots
1 cup semisweet chocolate chips
1 teaspoon peppermint extract
2 tablespoons unsalted butter, room temperature
2 teaspoons warm water
1 large candy cane, crushed

Directions:
- Preheat your oven to 425F. Use cooking spray to coat a baking sheet.
- Place the tater tots on the baking sheets.
- Bake the tots for 25 minutes. They should be nice and crispy.
- While the tots are cooking, put the butter, chocolate chips, and peppermint extract in a pan and heat on low heat until everything melts. Pour in the water and stir to thin out the mixture.
- Drizzle each tot with the chocolate icing, and top with candy cane pieces
- Serve the cooked tots immediately.

Chocolate Covered Tater Tots with Shredded Coconut

Prep Time: 15 Min. / **Cook Time:** 25 Min. / **Servings:** 8-10

Ingredients:
35 frozen tater tots
1 bag dark chocolate chips
½ cup shredded coconut

Directions:
- Preheat your oven to 425F. Use cooking spray to coat a baking sheet.
- Place the tater tots on the baking sheet.
- Bake the tots for 25 minutes. They should be golden brown when done.
- Line another baking sheet with parchment paper. Put 1 inch of water in a small pot and bring it to a boil on high heat. Pour the chocolate into a medium sized heat-proof bowl.
- Once the water is boiling, turn off the heat and place the bowl of chocolate on top. Stir the chocolate frequently until it's completely melted.
- Coat the tots with the chocolate and place them on the parchment paper lined baking sheet. Top with the shredded coconut.
- Put the baking sheet in the refrigerator for around 5 minutes until the chocolate cools and hardens.

Alicia Patterson

White Chocolate "Birthday Cake" Tater Tots

Prep Time: 15 Min. / **Cook Time:** 25 Min. / **Servings:** 8-10

Ingredients:
35 frozen tater tots
1 bag white chocolate chips
1 bottle of colored sprinkles

Directions:
- Preheat your oven to 425F. Use cooking spray to coat a baking sheet.
- Place the tater tots on the baking sheet.
- Bake the tots for 25 minutes. They should be golden brown when done.
- Line another baking sheet with parchment paper. Put 1 inch of water in a small pot and bring it to a boil on high heat. Pour the chocolate into a medium sized heat-proof bowl.
- Once the water is boiling, turn off the heat and place the bowl of chocolate on top. Stir the chocolate frequently until it's completely melted.
- Coat the tots with the chocolate and place them on the parchment paper lined baking sheet. Top with the sprinkles.
- Put the baking sheet in the refrigerator for around 5 minutes until the chocolate cools and hardens.

Cookies and Cream Tater Tots

Prep Time: 15 Min. / **Cook Time:** 25 Min. / **Servings:** 8-10

Ingredients:
35 frozen tater tots
1 bag white chocolate chips
About 10 sandwich cookies, crushed

Directions:
- Preheat your oven to 425F. Use cooking spray to coat a baking sheet.
- Place the tater tots on the baking sheet.
- Bake the tots for 25 minutes. They should be golden brown when done.
- Line another baking sheet with parchment paper. Put 1 inch of water in a small pot and bring it to a boil on high heat. Pour the chocolate into a medium sized heat-proof bowl.
- Once the water is boiling, turn off the heat and place the bowl of chocolate on top. Stir the chocolate frequently until it's completely melted.
- Coat the tots with the chocolate and place them on the parchment paper lined baking sheet. Coat with the sandwich cookies.
- Put the baking sheet in the refrigerator for around 5 minutes until the chocolate cools and hardens.

Peanut Butter Chocolate Tater Tots

Prep Time: 15 Min. / **Cook Time:** 25 Min. / **Servings:** 8-10

Ingredients:
35 frozen tater tots
1 bag dark chocolate chips
½ cup peanut butter chips

Directions:
- Preheat your oven to 425F. Use cooking spray to coat a baking sheet.
- Place the tater tots on the baking sheet.
- Bake the tots for 25 minutes. They should be golden brown when done.
- Line another baking sheet with parchment paper. Put 1 inch of water in a small pot and bring it to a boil on high heat. Pour the chocolate into a medium sized heat-proof bowl.
- Once the water is boiling, turn off the heat and place the bowl of chocolate on top. Stir the chocolate frequently until it's completely melted.
- Coat the tots with the chocolate and place them on the parchment paper lined baking sheet. Top with the peanut butter chips.
- Put the baking sheet in the refrigerator for around 5 minutes until the chocolate cools and hardens.

Chocolate Covered Tater Tots with Caramel and Sea Salt

Prep Time: 15 Min. / **Cook Time:** 25 Min. / **Servings:** 8-10

Ingredients:
35 frozen tater tots
1 bag dark chocolate chips
1 bottle caramel sauce
Flakey sea salt

Directions:
- Preheat your oven to 425F. Use cooking spray to coat a baking sheet.
- Place the tater tots on the baking sheet.
- Bake the tots for 25 minutes. They should be golden brown when done.
- Line another baking sheet with parchment paper. Put 1 inch of water in a small pot and bring it to a boil on high heat. Pour the chocolate into a medium sized heat-proof bowl.
- Once the water is boiling, turn off the heat and place the bowl of chocolate on top. Stir the chocolate frequently until it's completely melted.
- Coat the tots with the chocolate and place them on the parchment paper lined baking sheet. Drizzle with the caramel sauce and top with a little sea salt.
- Put the baking sheet in the refrigerator for around 5 minutes until the chocolate cools and hardens.

Alicia Patterson

White Chocolate Macadamia Nut Sweet Potato Tater Tots

Prep Time: 15 Min. / **Cook Time:** 27 Min. / **Servings:** 8-10

Ingredients:
35 frozen sweet potato tater tots
1 bag white chocolate chips
1/2 cup macadamia nuts, crushed

Directions:
- Preheat your oven to 425F. Use cooking spray to coat a baking sheet.
- Place the tater tots on the baking sheet.
- Bake the tots for 27 minutes. They should be golden brown when done.
- Line another baking sheet with parchment paper. Put 1 inch of water in a small pot and bring it to a boil on high heat. Pour the chocolate into a medium sized heat-proof bowl.
- Once the water is boiling, turn off the heat and place the bowl of chocolate on top. Stir the chocolate frequently until it's completely melted.
- Coat the tots with the chocolate and place them on the parchment paper lined baking sheet. Top with the macadamia nuts.
- Put the baking sheet in the refrigerator for around 5 minutes until the chocolate cools and hardens.

Milk Chocolate Pretzel Tater Tots

Prep Time: 15 Min. / **Cook Time:** 25 Min. / **Servings:** 8-10

Ingredients:
35 frozen tater tots
1 bag milk chocolate chips
1/2 cup pretzels, crushed

Directions:
- Preheat your oven to 425F. Use cooking spray to coat a baking sheet.
- Place the tater tots on the baking sheet.
- Bake the tots for 25 minutes. They should be golden brown when done.
- Line another baking sheet with parchment paper. Put 1 inch of water in a small pot and bring it to a boil on high heat. Pour the chocolate into a medium sized heat-proof bowl.
- Once the water is boiling, turn off the heat and place the bowl of chocolate on top. Stir the chocolate frequently until it's completely melted.
- Coat the tots with the chocolate and place them on the parchment paper lined baking sheet. Top with the pretzels.
- Put the baking sheet in the refrigerator for around 5 minutes until the chocolate cools and hardens.

Alicia Patterson

Dark Chocolate Almond Sweet Potato Tater Tots

Prep Time: 15 Min. / **Cook Time:** 27 Min. / **Servings:** 8-10

Ingredients:
35 frozen sweet potato tater tots
1 bag milk chocolate chips
1/2 cup almonds, crushed

Directions:
- Preheat your oven to 425F. Use cooking spray to coat a baking sheet.
- Place the tater tots on the baking sheet.
- Bake the tots for 27 minutes. They should be golden brown when done.
- Line another baking sheet with parchment paper. Put 1 inch of water in a small pot and bring it to a boil on high heat. Pour the chocolate into a medium sized heat-proof bowl.
- Once the water is boiling, turn off the heat and place the bowl of chocolate on top. Stir the chocolate frequently until it's completely melted.
- Coat the tots with the chocolate and place them on the parchment paper lined baking sheet. Top with the almonds.
- Put the baking sheet in the refrigerator for around 5 minutes until the chocolate cools and hardens.

S'mores Sweet Potato Tater Tots

Prep Time: 15 Min. / **Cook Time:** 27 Min. / **Servings:** 8-10

Ingredients:
35 frozen sweet potato tater tots
1 bag milk chocolate chips
1/4 cup graham crackers, crushed
1/4cup mini marshmallows, cut into small pieces

Directions:
- Preheat your oven to 425F. Use cooking spray to coat a baking sheet. Mix the graham crackers and mini marshmallows in a bowl.
- Place the tater tots on the baking sheet.
- Bake the tots for 27 minutes. They should be golden brown when done.
- Line another baking sheet with parchment paper. Put 1 inch of water in a small pot and bring it to a boil on high heat. Pour the chocolate into a medium sized heat-proof bowl.
- Once the water is boiling, turn off the heat and place the bowl of chocolate on top. Stir the chocolate frequently until it's completely melted.
- Coat the tots with the chocolate and place them on the parchment paper lined baking sheet. Coat with the graham cracker mixture.
- Put the baking sheet in the refrigerator for around 5 minutes until the chocolate cools and hardens.

Alicia Patterson

Dark Chocolate Pistachio Sweet Potato Tater Tots

Prep Time: 15 Min. / **Cook Time:** 27 Min. / **Servings:** 8-10

Ingredients:
35 frozen sweet potato tater tots
1 bag milk chocolate chips
1/2 cup pistachios, crushed

Directions:
- Preheat your oven to 425F. Use cooking spray to coat a baking sheet.
- Place the tater tots on the baking sheet.
- Bake the tots for 27 minutes. They should be golden brown when done.
- Line another baking sheet with parchment paper. Put 1 inch of water in a small pot and bring it to a boil on high heat. Pour the chocolate into a medium sized heat-proof bowl.
- Once the water is boiling, turn off the heat and place the bowl of chocolate on top. Stir the chocolate frequently until it's completely melted.
- Coat the tots with the chocolate and place them on the parchment paper lined baking sheet. Coat with the pistachios.
- Put the baking sheet in the refrigerator for around 5 minutes until the chocolate cools and hardens.

ABOUT OUR AUTHOR

Alicia Patterson is a southern girl from the heart of West Virginia that has a love for cooking in the kitchen. Growing up on a farm she quickly learned how to cook and prepare foods for a large family. Alicia started working at a restaurant and fell in love with it! Other restaurant owners soon learned how talented she was and she started teaching others how to cook like she did showing them how to enhance their menu items and pair foods together with their bar items, at the same time.

She has become a very well-known chef figure in the celebrity community. She has been working in the homes of many celebrities every-since. In her spare time, she loves jogging, horseback riding and reading. And of course, her love in the kitchen is on the first of the list.

"Hello and thank you for the purchase! I hope that this book captures your heart and give you more than enough ideas to what you can do with an air fryer! Enjoy!" Alicia Patterson, xoxo

Made in the USA
San Bernardino, CA
21 December 2019